BUMBLEBEE PAPERBACK EDITION

Copyright © Melanie Woolner 2021
Illustrations by Samantha Boyers

The right of Melanie Woolner to be identified as author of
this work has been asserted in accordance with sections 77 and 78 of the Copyright,
Designs and Patents Act 1988.

A CIP catalogue record for this title is
available from the British Library.

ISBN: 978-1-83934-293-6

Bumblebee Books is an imprint of
Olympia Publishers.

First Published in 2021

Bumblebee Books
Tallis House
2 Tallis Street
London
EC4Y 0AB

Printed in Great Britain

www.olympiapublishers.com

Melanie Woolner
Illustrations by Samantha Boyers

Keith's Teeth!

Bumblebee Books
London

Dedication

This book is dedicated to our wonderful families.

Keith O' Keef had a lot of teeth,
A lot of teeth had Keith O' Keef!

Keith O' Keef had wobbly teeth,
Lots of wobbly teeth had Keith O' Keef!

Keith O' Keef lost all his teeth,
Lost all his teeth did Keith O' Keef!

Keith O' Keef wrapped up his teeth,
Wrapped up his teeth did Keith O' Keef!

Keith O' Keef hid his teeth,
He hid his teeth did Keith O' Keef!

Keith O' Keef went to sleep,
He went to sleep did Keith O' Keef!

Keith O' Keef heard a noise,
He heard a noise did Keith O' Keef!

Keith O' Keef got a surprise,
He got a surprise did Keith O' Keef!

Keith O' Keef had lots of new teeth,
Lots of new teeth had Keith O' Keef!

About the Author

I love writing stories, poems, anything that can be written down from my imagination. I have always thought up stories from being very young and love how they give us little glimpses into our lives and those of others.